Step by Step

# The Story of an Apple

## It Starts with a Seed

Stacy Taus-Bolstad

Lerner Publications ◆ Minneapolis

Lerner Publications Company
An imprint of Lerner Publishing Group, Inc.
241 First Avenue North
Minneapolis, MN 55401 USA

For reading levels and more information, look up this title at www.lernerbooks.com.

Image credits: kali9/Getty Images, p. 3; rupaite/Shutterstock.com, pp. 5, 23 (top right); AnaFidalgo/iStockphoto/Getty Images, p. 7; krolya25/Shutterstock.com, pp. 9, 23 (bottom left); Adam Gryko/Shutterstock.com, pp. 11, 23 (top left); Anna V. Ponomareva/Getty Images, p. 13; Chelmicky/Shutterstock.com, p. 15; Eugene Kovalchuk/Shutterstock.com, p. 17; Vesna Andjic/E+/Getty Images, pp. 19, 23 (bottom right); Donald Iain Smith/Getty Images, p. 21; cometary/Getty Images, p. 22. Cover: xxmmxx/E+/Getty Images; Garsya/iStock/Getty Images.

Main body text set in Mikado a Medium.
Typeface provided by HVD Fonts.

**Editor:** Alison Lorenz **Designer:** Lauren Cooper
**Lerner team:** Andrea Nelson

**Library of Congress Cataloging-in-Publication Data**

Names: Taus-Bolstad, Stacy, author.
Title: The story of an apple : it starts with a seed / Stacy Taus-Bolstad.
Description: Minneapolis : Lerner Publications, 2021 | Series: Step by step | Includes bibliographical references and index. | Audience: Ages 4–8 | Audience: Grades K–1 | Summary: "A seed grows into a tasty apple. But how? Engaging photos and straightforward text guide readers step by step"—Provided by publisher.
Identifiers: LCCN 2019045808 (print) | LCCN 2019045809 (ebook) | ISBN 9781541597754 (library binding) | ISBN 9781728401096 (ebook)
Subjects: LCSH: Apples—Juvenile literature.
Classification: LCC SB363 .T296 2021 (print) | LCC SB363 (ebook) | DDC 634/.11—dc23

LC record available at https://lccn.loc.gov/2019045808
LC ebook record available at https://lccn.loc.gov/2019045809

Manufactured in the United States of America
2-53625-48366-7/6/2022

Apples taste good! How do they grow?

3

A farmer
plants seeds.

# The seeds change.

The trees get big.

Flowers open.

The flowers fall.

Small apples grow
on the trees.

The apples change.

Workers pick
the apples.

People buy
the apples.

# Crunch!